I Can Make a Friend

By Melissa H. Mwai

Copyright © 2025 WonderLab Group LLC
Published by Paw Prints Publishing
A division of Baker & Taylor
Paw Prints Publishing and associated logos are trademarks and/or registered trademarks of Baker & Taylor.
All rights reserved. No part of this book may be reproduced or used in any matter without written permission of the copyright owner except for the use of quotations in a book review.
ISBN: 978-1-2231-8875-1 (paperback)
ISBN: 978-1-2231-8876-8 (reinforced library binding)

Library of Congress Cataloging-in-Publication Data available.

For information about special sales and premium purchases, please contact specialsales@btpubservices.com.
www.PawPrintsPublishing.com
Printed in China

Created and produced by WonderLab Group LLC

Written by Melissa H. Mwai
Series Consulting Editor: Alexa Patrick
Design by Fan Works Design LLC
Photo research by Annette Kiesow

Be sure to check with an adult before you begin a new project!

Image credits:
Key: bk=background, Shutterstock = Sh
All illustrations by yusufdemirci/Shutterstock unless otherwise noted.
Cover: Steve Debenport/iStock/Getty Images, (bk) yusufdemirci/Sh.1: FatCamera/iStock/E+/Getty Images; 2: Robert Kneschke/Sh; 4: thebigland/Sh; 6: SeventyFour/Sh; 7 (bk): JameSit/Sh; 8 (bk), 9 (bk): Ground Picture/Sh; 10-11: ZUMA Press Inc/Alamy; 12 (bk): ViDI Studio/Sh; 14: Teerawat Anothaistaporn/Sh; 15, 30 (lo): Monkey Business Images/Sh; 16: NotionPic/Sh; 17 (bk): Susan B Sheldon/Sh; 19: ShineTerra/Sh; 20 (caps): White studio/Sh; 20 (bk): Sombat S/Sh; 21 (up): monticello/Sh, 21 (bench): a_v_d/Sh 21 (bk): Naypong Studio/Sh; 22-23 (bk): Andrus Ciprian/Sh; 24: Sergey Novikov/Sh; 25: vik.stock/Sh; 26 (child): lapetitelumiere/Sh; 26 (adult): 9nong/Sh; 26 (bk): gyn9037/Sh; 27 (bk): Kwangmoozaa/Sh; 28: ESB Professional/Sh; 30 (up): Orion Production/Sh.

Table of Contents

What Are Friends? 4

You Can Be Kind 6

You Can Ask 14

You Can Help 22

Glossary 30

I Can Do It Pledge 32

What Are Friends?

Bestie. Buddy. BFF. No matter what you call them, we enjoy spending time with our friends.

It may take time to make a friend.

At first you may know only a few things about a person. This makes you **acquaintances**.

Maybe you see them around the neighborhood or at school.

Maybe you like some of the same things. Maybe you have the same **hobbies**.

A friendship is born.

You Can Be Kind

A friend spends time with you. They treat you kindly. Friends help each other. These are all things good friends do.

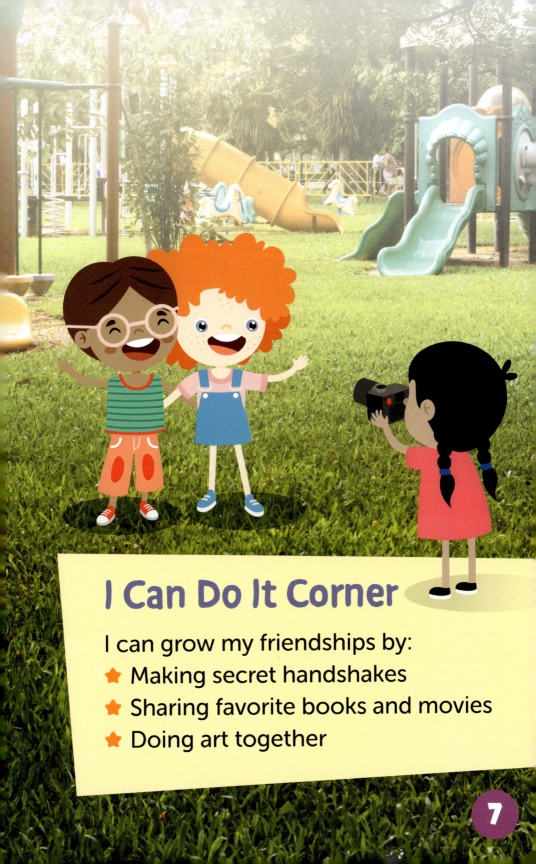

I Can Do It Corner

I can grow my friendships by:
- ⭐ Making secret handshakes
- ⭐ Sharing favorite books and movies
- ⭐ Doing art together

What Is Bullying?

Not all people treat each other kindly. Sometimes, people are mean to others. They are mean on purpose. They are a **bully**.

A bully might leave a person out of a game. Or stop someone from doing what they want. A bully might say mean words. Or do unkind things.

If you see bullying happen to someone, say something. Tell a grown-up.

The best way to stop bullying is by being kind.

I Can Do It Corner

I can be kind by:
- Saying hello to someone new
- Starting a friendship club
- Asking a sad person if they are okay

Unity Day

Kids stand up to bullies on **Unity** Day. Unity Day is a day in October. Kids wear orange to show that no one should be bullied. They talk about why it is important to be kind.

I Can Do It Corner

Does your school celebrate Unity Day?
- ⭐ Yes: Find a way to help get ready for Unity Day.
- ⭐ No: Share the idea with a teacher.

Medha's Super Skills

Medha knew about Unity Day. She wanted to stand up to bullies in her school. She used the computer a lot. How could Medha use her super skills to help others?

Medha made a video about Unity Day. She posted the video online.

Always ask a grown-up before going online!

Many kids watched her video. They learned about Unity Day, too.

I Can Imagine It

Have you seen someone be unkind?
Why would you want to stop bullying?

You Can Ask

Some friends love recess games. Others just talk and walk. If you are shy, joining can be hard.

It can be easier to make a friend if someone asks you to join them.

The Best Bench

Christian saw a special playground bench. It was called a buddy bench. Kids could sit here if they felt lonely. Then others could ask them to play or talk.

Christian wanted a buddy bench at his school, too. He met with the principal. They got a bench for their playground.

Kids used it to make friends.

I Can Imagine It

Imagine meeting someone shy at recess. What would you say to them?

The Big Hit

One day, the news wrote about Christian's bench. The idea took off!

Other schools wanted buddy benches, too. Christian spoke on TV. He told other kids about the benches.

I Can Do It Corner

Does your school have a buddy bench?
⭐ Yes: Use it and tell other kids.
⭐ No: Where would you put one? Find someone who could help you!

This Kid Did It!

Calling All Kids

Sammie heard about buddy benches. She started a new project. Sammie and her mom found a company that made benches from bottle caps.

Building one bench took 400 pounds of bottle caps.

Sammie talked to the kids in her school. They collected caps.

The kids gave over 1600 pounds of caps! They built three benches for Sammie's school.

You Can Help

Friends are helpers. Friends make scary feelings like finding a lunch buddy easier. Friends look out for each other.

Medha's video helped more kids find out about Unity Day.

Kids look out for one another on Unity Day or any day someone needs help!

Just Ask

Sometimes, all it takes to make a friend is asking a person to play. That can make someone feel like they belong. And you make a new friend at the same time!

That was the idea behind buddy benches. Schools all around the world use the benches now.

Think of all the friendships made because of those benches!

This Kid Did It!

High-Five Friend

Friends can be different. Having **diverse** friends gives you a chance to try different things. They might think in a different way.

Fiona had a friend who was different from her. She called him "High Five" because he gave her a high five.

Every Saturday, Fiona went to the market with her mom. It was time to say hello to High Five. He worked at the market.

Fiona and her mom did not know their buddy's real name: Gilnet. He was almost 50! That did not matter.

They high-fived every week. That was what mattered most.

You Can Make a Friend, Too!

Think of ways you could be kind to someone. This could be someone in school. Or it could be someone in your neighborhood.

- ⭐ Write them a letter or make them a card showing them how great they are.
- ⭐ Think of one thing you like about them and tell them.
- ⭐ Ask them if they need help with something. Then do it with them.

Share your idea with a grown-up. Not sure what to do to be kind? No problem. Be like Sammie and Christian. Sit with someone new!

Glossary

Acquaintances: (uh-KWAYN-tuhn-suhz) people who are friendly but know very little about each other.

Bully: (bu-LEE) a person who teases or hurts someone else on pupose.

Diverse: (dy-VURS) different from each other.

Hobbies: (hob-EES) fun interests or activities.

Unity: (YOO-nuh-tee) working together to do something hard or big.

I Can Do It Pledge

Now you have read about friendship. Grab a sheet of paper and make a sign. Write about what YOU will do. Use this pledge as a guide.

I Can Do It

_____ (Your Name) is an I Can Do it Kid!

_____ (Your Name) did _____ (1 thing)

to help _____ (pick one: self, family, school, community, or world)

on _____ (date) be more

(pick something positive: awesome, friendly, full of kindness ...)
_____ .